CYCLING

BY ASHLEY GISH

CREATIVE EDUCATION • CREATIVE PAPERBACKS

Published by Creative Education and Creative Paperbacks
P.O. Box 227, Mankato, Minnesota 56002
Creative Education and Creative Paperbacks are imprints of
The Creative Company
www.thecreativecompany.us

Design by The Design Lab
Production by Alison Derry
Art direction by Tom Morgan
Edited by Alissa Thielges

Photographs by Getty Images (Anne-Christine Poujoulat, ANP, Doug
Pensinger, Elsa, Hulton Archive, Jasper Jacobs, Justin Setterfield, Kyodo News,
Peter Parks, Richard Baker, Shirlaine Forrest, Tim Clayton – Corbis, Michał
Chodyra), Shutterstock (DELOYS)

Library of Congress Cataloging-in-Publication Data
Names: Gish, Ashley, author.
Title: Cycling / by Ashley Gish.
Description: [Mankato, Minnesota] : [Creative Education and Creative
    Paperbacks], [2024] | Series: Amazing Summer Olympics | Includes
    bibliographical references and index. | Audience: Ages 6–9 years |
    Audience: Grades 2–3 | Summary: "Celebrate the Summer Olympic Games
    with this elementary-level introduction to cycling, the sport known for speed
    and endurance on bikes. Includes biographical facts about BMX cyclist
    and gold medalist Charlotte Worthington"—Provided by publisher.
Identifiers: LCCN 2023007957 (print) | LCCN 2023007958 (ebook) |
    ISBN 9781640267633 (library binding) | ISBN 9781682773130
    (paperback) | ISBN 9781640009332 (pdf)
Subjects: LCSH: Cycling—Juvenile literature. | Summer Olympics—Juvenile
    literature. | Worthington, Charlotte—Juvenile literature. | Mountain
    biking—Juvenile literature. | Stunt cycling—Juvenile literature. |
    Bicycle motocross—Juvenile literature. | BMX freestyle (Stunt
    cycling)—Juvenile literature.
Classification: LCC GV1043.5 .G575 2024 (print) | LCC GV1043.5 (ebook)
    | DDC 796.6—dc23/eng/20230310
LC record available at https://lccn.loc.gov/2023007957
LC ebook record available at https://lccn.loc.gov/2023007958

Table of Contents

Cycling has been in the Summer Olympics since 1896. Road and track racing came first. Mountain biking was added in 1996. BMX racing was introduced to the Olympics in 2008. All of these events use different types of bikes.

The Great Britain team won gold in a team cycling event in 1908.

Road courses include hills to further challenge racers.

Road cycling takes place outside on paved roads. Cyclists all start at the same time. They race against each other. They need lots of **endurance**. Men race 124 miles (200 kilometers). Women race 75 miles (121 km). The first three racers to cross the finish line win a medal.

endurance the ability to go continuously without wearing down

The road race events at Tokyo 2020 ended at the base of Mount Fuji.

Time trials also take place on an open road. Cyclists start one at a time. They don't race against each other. They race against the clock. Men pedal 27.5 miles (44.3 km). Women race half that distance. The three best times win medals.

Cyclists use aero handlebars to ride low and fast.

The shape of the track allows cyclists to gain speed quickly.

Track cycling happens on a velodrome. Sprint races last three laps. Riders reach explosive speeds. By the third lap, they may be going 43 miles (69 km) per hour! Track bikes have solid disk wheels, only one gear, and no brakes.

lap a full circle around a track

velodrome an oval-shaped racing arena with sloped sides for track cycling

The omnium consists of four races in one day.

Endurance events take place on the track, too. In the omnium, cyclists earn points based on how well they do in four different races. In team pursuit, two teams of four riders race over 16 laps. Teammates **draft** each other in a single line to save energy. They try to finish first or catch up to the other team.

draft to ride close behind another bicycle to benefit from the drop in air pressure created behind it

Helmets and pads protect cyclists in crashes.

The Madison is a tag-team track cycling event. A team of two riders takes turns resting and racing. When it's time to switch, the teammates grab each other's hand. One rider slings the other forward for a burst of speed.

Hand-slings and pushes help teammates pass or stay ahead of opponents.

Mountain bikes handle rough, bumpy trails and big drops without breaking.

Mountain bikers race on dirt roads. The winding path often cuts through forests. Cyclists travel through a natural **obstacle** course made of rocks and logs. Steep hills slow racers down. But then they zoom down the other side.

obstacle an object to go over or around

BMX races happen on special dirt tracks. There are bumps, jumps, and banked turns. Cyclists wear full-face helmets, a jersey, and long pants. Freestyle BMX came to the Olympics at Tokyo 2020. Racers use ramps to fly into the air. They earn points by doing flips, spins, and other stunts in 60 seconds.

BMX cyclists may reach speeds of up to 37 miles (60 km) per hour.

Olympic cycling has something for everyone. It is fun to guess who will win a long road race. Don't look away from a track sprint—any cyclist could win in an instant. Mountain biking and BMX events are thrilling to watch. Each athlete tries their best to win the gold!

Jason Kenny (blue) of Great Britain is the most decorated Olympic cyclist.

Competitor Spotlight: Charlotte Worthington

British cyclist Charlotte Worthington first learned how to perform bike tricks on a scooter. She discovered BMX as a teen. She worked as a chef while competing in BMX competitions. By age 25, she was the first woman to win gold in BMX Freestyle at Tokyo 2020. Her greatest wish is to inspire girls and young women to join this exciting sport.

Read More

De Medeiros, Michael. *Mountain Biking.* New York: Lightbox Learning, 2023.

Hale, K. A. *BMX Racing.* Minnetonka, Minn.: Kaleidoscope, 2019.

Websites

Cycling
https://kids.britannica.com/kids/article/cycling/353027
Learn more about cycling.

Cycling
https://www.dkfindout.com/us/sports/cycling/
Learn about different parts of a bicycle.

Cycling at the Tokyo Olympic Games
https://www.nbcolympics.com/news/cycling-tokyo-olympic-games
Read about cycling events and rules from Tokyo 2020.

Note: Every effort has been made to ensure that the websites listed above are suitable for children, that they have educational value, and that they contain no inappropriate material. However, because of the nature of the Internet, it is impossible to guarantee that these sites will remain active indefinitely or that their contents will not be altered.

Index